Guide for Asset Integrity Managers

A Comprehensive Guide to Strategies, Practices and Benchmarking

AF797658

Dr. Zaid Fayyaz

pencil

ISBN 978-93-5458-331-5
© Dr. Zaid Fayyaz 2021
Published in India 2021 by Pencil

A brand of
One Point Six Technologies Pvt. Ltd.
123, Building J2, Shram Seva Premises,
Wadala Truck Terminal, Wadala (E)
Mumbai 400037, Maharashtra, INDIA
E connect@thepencilapp.com
W www.thepencilapp.com

All rights reserved worldwide

No part of this publication may be reproduced, stored in or introduced into a retrieval system, or transmitted, in any form, or by any means (electronic, mechanical, photocopying, recording or otherwise), without the prior written permission of the Publisher. Any person who commits an unauthorized act in relation to this publication can be liable to criminal prosecution and civil claims for damages.

DISCLAIMER: *The opinions expressed in this book are those of the authors and do not purport to reflect the views of the Publisher.*

CONTENTS

Guide for Asset Integrity Managers.. 5

Guide for Asset Integrity Managers

Guide for Asset Integrity Managers

A Comprehensive Guide to Strategies, Practices and Benchmarking

Introduction

Asset Integrity Management (AIM) is a term used to describe the practice of managing an asset (power plant, oil rig, refinery, etc) to ensure its ability to perform its function effectively and efficiently is maintained. Well run AIM strategies ensure that the people, systems, processes and resources that enable an asset to deliver its function are in place over the life cycle of the asset, while simultaneously maintaining health and safety and environmental legislation. AIM applies to the entirety of an asset's operation, from its design phase to its decommissioning and replacement.

The primary industry sector served by AIM is upstream oil and gas. This is owing to the escalating worldwide demand for energy, which has resulted in the oil and gas sector increasing investment into this area to extend the operational service life of existing rigs. However, the AIM process can be implemented for any asset of high value, including oil refineries, electrical power generation plants and chemical processing plants.

Drivers for asset management

If infrastructure assets are not delivered or made available in the most cost effective manner, society will bear unnecessary costs and may make decisions it would not have made otherwise, or suffer other adverse consequences. The principal drivers that lead to adopting and continued development of AM practices are society's desires for:

Improved governance of and accountability for its essential infrastructure

Enhanced service management and customer satisfaction

Improved risk management

Improved financial efficiency

Sustainable management of assets, resources and the environment.

Know how the organisation is performing –operations performance management

Both operational and organisational performance are quite distinct from asset performance. For example, a network might be in excellent condition and running at the lowest lifecycle cost but customer calls are not answered, internal and external reporting deadlines are not met and statutory information is not provided.

Most organisations have LoS, which can (confusingly) also be called Customer LoS, that state the desired performances in these areas. These Customer Service LoS and Reporting LoS must be reflected in the Customer LoS and Technical LoS agreed for inclusion in the AMP and in the day to day management practices for the assets.

Role of Asset Integrity Engineer

Asset Integrity Engineers focus on ensuring that an asset will perform its desired function over its life cycle. A constant challenge for AIM engineers is to balance the designing, maintenance and replacement of assets throughout their life cycle, while minimising costs to business in terms of finance, time and resources.

AIM engineers are required to conduct many tasks, including:

Implement condition and structural health monitoring (CSM)

Ensure inspection intervals are not exceeded

Perform risk-based inspection (RBI)

Conduct life extension studies

Perform fitness-for-service reviews

Conduct failure investigation studies

Monitor and ensure procedures are maintained and implemented

Participate in preparation of capital and operating budgets for inspection

Pipeline Integrity Management

Pipelines are a crucial part of the energy delivery system. The oil and gas industry and its supply chain invest heavily to ensure that pipelines continue to meet the needs of the energy industry worldwide.

Pipeline integrity management (PIM) is the philosophy of implementing a cradle-to-grave approach of understanding and operating pipelines in a safe, reliable manner [3]. Pipeline operators need a pipeline integrity management solution which is able to store and integrate critical data about the pipeline route, materials, facilities, operations, inspections, repairs and modifications to ensure efficient through-life operational efficiency.

Pipeline operators are required to abide by regulations that require regular baseline evaluations of pipelines in areas where failures are most likely to occur and result in significant detrimental impact on public safety or the environment.

What does asset integrity mean for the oil and gas industry?

Asset integrity, or asset integrity management systems (AIMS) is the term for an asset's capacity to run effectively and accurately, whilst also protecting the wellbeing of all personnel and equipment with which it interacts – as well as the measures in place to assure the asset's life cycle. Asset integrity applies to the entirety of an assets operation, from its design phase to its decommissioning and replacement.

The constant business challenge for asset integrity managers is how to balance the designing, maintenance, and replacement of assets throughout their life cycle with the costs to business – in terms of finance, time, and resources. At its heart, it is the managing of the degradation of assets.

6.1. Elements of asset integrity management

Much of the oil and gas industry's infrastructure is now either approaching or ageing far past its operational life expectancy. With the cost of replacing assets, and the resultant turnaround time, prohibitively high for so many facilities, asset integrity is now rivalling terms such as OPEX and Agile as the watchword on people's lips.

Challenges such as vessel inspection, which is a significant contributing factor to production downtime, and corrosion under insulation, a frequent cause of sudden shutdowns, are on the rise – and taking the step to employ new solutions is becoming a necessity in many sites, particularly those offshore.

6.2. The human element

Asset integrity is built on a belief that the majority of people within the company will do things properly, and however optimistic that may sound, most of the time maintenance, inspection, and data management is conducted with the best of intentions. However, things are often not completed thoroughly or in as timely a manner as possible. Simple solutions like more frequent inspections won't necessarily scoop up every missed issue, nor will it engender a spirit of enthusiasm if workers are asked to increase their inspection work, or implicated in faults that are missed.

Some signs that things may not all be well in the world of asset integrity management and inspection can include:
Team members feel like any concerns they have about health and safety or the state of equipment are not being taken seriously, leading to an environment in which faults are not even reported
Any changes made to asset integrity plans, or even basic running of the facility, only occur after a large-scale incident
A lack of understanding around how to find root causes from simple fault reports, often resulting in people being lulled into a false sense of security and overstating the level to which the facility is safe and operational
There is a reliance on tacit understanding, rather than a tangible and easily-accessible set of rules surrounding AIM and reporting faults
There is a lowest-bidder attitude surrounding maintenance contractors, and knowledge of and enthusiasm for asset integrity isn't valued particularly highly
The very real result of this sort of climate is that nothing

really happens. Asset integrity remains a barely tolerable nuisance – a sort of roadblock to proper work, until a major incident forces a company to adapt, often at great cost.

Plugging the gaps in asset integrity management systems

Whilst there are more AIM systems on the market than at any other point in the past, there are still no out-of-the-box catch-all solutions. No inspection plan or database can deal with all the AIM issues that can arise, but integrity systems are still seen as separate to the rest of operations. Staff can be unwilling to take ownership of their responsibilities, instead seeing the suite of various AIM packages as an attempt by the company to police them, rather than an integral part of their role.

The gaps in AIM packages need to be filled with the vigilance of the very people they are designed to protect, but a novel approach may be necessary to ensure this message is heard.

Why asset integrity management is important

Over the course of 22 minutes on July 6th 1988, the Piper Alpha North Sea oil platform leaked condensed gas that ignited and led to an explosion killing 167 of the rig's 229 workers. This disaster is seen by many of the formative moment of modern approaches to both EH&S and AIM in oil and gas, not least because it led to a £1 billion safety measure investment from every offshore operator.

The UK government then followed up with a public inquiry which came to fruition in 1990, and contained 106 directions on how better to conduct HS&E and AIM strategies in future – all of which were accepted by the oil and gas industry.

So, now that we are living and working in an age of serious AIM efforts, which areas should people be focussing on?

Constructing an AIM strategy

Based on research conducted by Oil & Gas IQ, oil and gas operators are now engaging in price-responsive strategies and the optimisation of existing assets. In the North Sea in particular, these companies are now re-evaluating their practices in order to make ends meet. 51 per cent of oil and gas professionals are now working on installations over 20 years into their service lives – with less than a third working on installations in their first decade of service.

More than half of asset integrity professionals have had their budgets cut and the average chosen rating of those professionals own companies AIM rating was 5.4 out of ten. Only 52 per cent thought that their job load was sustainable with regards to meeting targets and maintaining safety – and the majority only had a meagre budget of less than £250,000. Unsurprisingly, the two greatest issues according to those in asset integrity are managing assets in budget and the age of the assets themselves. By far the greatest flaw perceived in oil and gas companies is the lack of communication between departments, followed by a lack of safety culture. Work to be done, indeed.

RBI: risk-based inspection

With ageing infrastructure fast becoming one of the industry's major concerns, it is more important than ever to make sure an effective system of identification is in place. More than half of the pipelines in the US are at least 50 years old, with 3,300 leaks, including the largest in US pipeline history, eighty deaths, and nearly 400 injuries, in the past five years alone. Despite it sounding somewhat obvious, managing integrity, corrosion, and damage is like scoping out an iceberg from some distance away.

For every easily-identifiable symptom of corrosion or asset instability, there are dozens of hidden issues: hydrogen attack, high-temperature tempering, thermal fatigue, metallurgy issues, internal system corrosion, and so on – and without dedicated and experienced professionals, implementing damage mitigation techniques is next to impossible. Once one has identified the need for thorough inspection, the next step is to enact it.

RBI, or risk-based inspection is one such method – whereby one must balance risk reduction with the minimum amount of effort required to streamline the process and free up more time. However, there are a near-infinite number of ways in which to carry our maintenance – and with many risks (such as calibration uncertainty or equipment accessibility) quantification is simply not possible. Therefore, each company must decide how far along the quantitative/qualitative scale it sits; whether to rely more heavily on experts, or statistics.

Depending on how well or badly a company nurtures its reliability culture, it will be operating in either a reactive or a proactive manner. Needless to say, you want be proactive. Failure to anticipate and monitor for hidden issues means you can only respond once problems have escalated, costing far more in the long run, and rewarding those who are shown to be able to react quickly. Far from improving the culture, this positive reinforcement further encourages reaction over action.

dentifying damage conditions - and the factors that alter them

To nobody's surprise, increasing the temperature of the environment in which an asset is located will significantly increase the rate of degradation. But so too will localising your asset in a halogen-rich environment, or failing to identify a spike in trace compounds such as chlorides or hydroxides – or any high- or low- pH material.

Even a small but consistent stream of air into a fuel stream will damage pipelines, far more than either carbon dioxide and hydrogen sulphide.

Here are a few other particularly doom-laden combinations that anyone seriously committed to ensuring asset integrity should be aware of – from lead contamination in water, to nickel in acidic conditions. The majority, however, can be improved by ensuring clean and precise operations – as many damaging combinations do not occur naturally. Believe it or not, steel rigs in seawater don't last forever, hence the rise in specialist coating vendors in the past couple of decades.

The third factor we need to consider in order to fully comprehend damage mechanism as best we can, is that of basic strain. Basic strain is when you factor in the stress inherent to the operation (as if it were operating in an ideal world).

We won't bore you with a full run-down of the sort of things to expect in every oil and gas operation – you can, but failure to fully identify your damage mechanisms may result in you developing a AIM strategy that can compound your issues rather than solve them. Think of it as like taking the right medication for the wrong condition.

Application of Asset Integrity Management

AIM are used manage the capability of an asset to perform its required function throughout the asset's lifecycle. The systems help ensure that the people, systems, processes, and resources that deliver integrity are in place, in use and will perform when required.

Asset integrity is managed at each stage of the asset lifecycle, including project design, asset operation and decommissioning. Inspections, auditing/assurance and overall quality processes are just some of the means to execute an effective integrity management program. A program can include:

Risk Based Inspection strategy

Pipeline integrity management typically for corrosion

In-service inspection with routine and specialist non-destructive testing

Reliability centred maintenance (RCM)

Condition-based maintenance

Vibration induced fatigue failure solutions

The AIM is used to maintain the asset in a fit-for-service condition while extending its remaining life span in a reliable, safe and cost-effective manner. In the US, AIM programs are deployed to meet API-580, API-581, and PAS 55 requirements.

An asset integrity management system does not exist in isolation. To successfully implement an asset integrity management system in a dynamic operating environment, it is essential that all stakeholders have a consistent and a unified understanding of what the essentials of asset integrity are and how they can be applied in their day-to-day operations, yet this is often cited as among the most significant challenges in achieving an integrity culture within an organization

Fundamentals of Asset Integrity Management

In a post-Macondo world, the role of asset integrity has never been more critical to the global oil and gas business. Not only can a well-managed asset integrity programme help operators identify and reduce safety risks before they escalate, but focusing on asset integrity can also play a major role in both achieving operational excellence and extending the life of ageing assets.

The asset integrity challenge:
This in itself is nothing new, but if the industry agrees that the benefits of asset integrity are clear, and if it now accepts that it is business-critical, what makes it so difficult, and how can those who are responsible for ensuring asset integrity overcome the inhibitors to achieving lasting integrity success?
Operators agree that the key to being able to achieve success is ensuring that every individual with a stake in asset integrity truly understands the core concepts invovled in effective integrity mangagement and how their actions and decisions can have a decisive impact on a company's ability to operate safely and efficiently.

The asset integrity solution:
From organisational integrity, through risk management, all the way to corrosion, reliability and integrity implementation, this unique Series of online Training Courses will unlock the keys to truly understanding the fundamentals of asset integrity to everyone with a stake in this business-critical subject.
The five Courses in this Series are equally suited for either (a) new entrants to the business who need to get up to speed on this important area, (b) current practitioners operating across disciplines who need to quickly ensure they are familiar with what may be new concepts, or (c) those who are looking for a primer in some of the

fundamental concepts of this key industry focus.
The courses assume no existing knowledge of this subject, this Series of online training courses is perfect for those with a need to get up to speed in the fastest, most effective and most flexible way possible.

Why Asset Integrity Management Matters
An effective Mechanical / Asset Integrity program provides assurance that a facility's equipment and assets are designed, fabricated, procured, installed and maintained in a manner appropriate for its intended application, throughout the life of the operation. As a risk management program, asset integrity management (AIM) focuses on the core elements of safety, environmental protection, reliability, regulatory compliance and data management.
Our risk based approach to managing asset integrity addresses improving efficiency, increasing uptime and reducing both operational costs and risk. A robust AIM solution helps owners/operators optimize the service life and operational performance of existing assets.
Fixed Equipment Inspection and Certification
In order to protect their licenses to operate, facility owners must verify that their in-service equipment demonstrates the appropriate levels of safety, integrity and reliability. Operators set annual targets to maintain maximum production and avoid unnecessary downtime due to mechanical failure or loss of integrity. To support these objectives, maintaining equipment documentation facilitates better management of safer, more reliable and compliant assets and operations.
Corrosion Under Insulation

Operators are seeking the most advanced and data-driven technical solutions to support a full lifecycle approach for controlling the risk of corrosion. Corrosion management and AIM should be integrated as part of an overall cost-effective maintenance effort that optimizes service life, safety and operational performance. Corrosion under Insulation (CUI) is a pervasive damage mechanism that affects almost every facility in the world. ABS Group can help facility owners minimize CUI failures and increase operational efficiency by effectively organizing and executing a CUI implementation program.

What Is Transportation Asset Management?

Asset management in the transportation industry is a relatively new concept. It means many things to many organizations, but its practices provide a solid foundation for programs that optimize the performance and cost-effectiveness of transportation facilities. At its core, asset management is a business process. The application of asset management principles often means a change in thinking at every level in an organization: to base decisions on information and on getting results.

The roots of today's asset management programs originated in private industry, integrating many of the ideas of W. Edwards Demming, Malcolm Baldridge, and others. Because of its focus, asset management has been highly successful in companies that require a substantial asset base for their operations, such as electrical power companies, telephone companies, large trucking companies, and railroads. In these companies, the goal was clear-maintain a prescribed level of service at the lowest cost possible. Assets that did not meet these criteria were taken out of service and sold. This focus on guaranteeing an acceptable level of service to the customer has had positive results and has made substantial profits for these companies.

Elected officials and public agency managers noted these advancements in the private sector and began to identify ways that government could be run as a business. Although profit is not a motive in the public sector, the basic concepts of performance and cost-effectiveness apply to virtually all government activities. In addition, the sheer investment in transportation assets owned and operated by public agencies is enormous-over $1.75 trillion. In 1993, the U.S. Congress passed the Government Performance and Results Act,1 legislation that identified accountability at all levels in the Federal Government as a priority. Many States have enacted similar legislation, typically calling for State agencies to report what is bought with public funds, how spending decisions are made, and what is accomplished. For transportation agencies, this means a full and updated accounting of the public assets-roads, bridges, and other facilities-that form the basis of Transportation Asset Management.

Defining Transportation Asset Management

Although defining asset management in the private sector was a straightforward process, for the transportation community, it has been somewhat of a struggle. Early definitions identified strategic management as the goal and were often all-inclusive in their descriptions, but they were not always sufficiently focused to be useful working definitions.

An asset management decisionmaking framework needs to

be guided by performance goals, cover an extended time horizon, draw from economics as well as engineering, and consider a broad range of assets. At its most basic level, Transportation Asset Management links user expectations for system condition, performance, and availability with system management and investment strategies. Regardless of the definition, the focus is on performance of assets. The underlying goal of asset management is to take a broad approach to resource allocation and programming decisions that will provide greater value to the system and overall satisfaction for end usersthrough improvements in program effectiveness and system performance. The core principles of asset management are listed in the box at right.

Transportation Asset Management provides for a fact-based dialogue among system users and other stakeholders, State government officials, and managers concerned with day-to-day operations. This dialogue results when relevant, objective, and credible information is made accessible to all participants in the decisionmaking process. As such, decisions can be based on detailed input regarding available resources, current system condition and performance, and estimates of future performance. The information underlying asset management-sometimes raw data and at other times data generated from the analytical process-is fundamental to an improved understanding of the economic tradeoffs, return on investment, and potential value of the end product.

The Core Principles of Asset Management

Policy-driven-Resource allocation decisions are based on a well-defined set of policy goals and objectives.

Performance-based-Policy objectives are translated into

system performance measures that are used for both day-to-day and strategic management.

Analysis of Options and Tradeoffs-Decisions on how to allocate funds within and across different types of investments (e.g., preventive maintenance versus rehabilitation, pavements versus bridges) are based on an analysis of how different allocations will impact achievement of relevant policy objectives.

Decisions Based on Quality Information-The merits of different options with respect to an agency's policy goals are evaluated using credible and current data.

Monitoring Provides Clear Accountability and Feedback-Performance results are monitored and reported for both impacts and effectiveness

The Federal Highway Association (FHWA), with leadership from the Office of Asset Management, partners with the American Association of State Highway and Transportation Officials (AASHTO), State and local departments of transportation (DOTs) along with FHWA field offices, the Transportation Research Board, and industry in encouraging the application of asset management. As defined by the AASHTO Standing Committee on Highways, Planning Subcommittee on Asset Management,

Transportation Asset Management is a strategic and systematic process of operating, maintaining, upgrading, and expanding physical assets effectively throughout their lifecycle. It focuses on business and engineering practices for resource allocation and utilization, with the objective of better decision making based upon quality information and well defined objectives.2

Over the years, a number of management systems derived

from the private sector have been adopted by transportation agencies with varying degrees of success. Some of these include management by objectives, goal-oriented management, risk-based management, and, more recently, enterprise resource planning (ERP). Asset management has many similarities to these methods and incorporates some of the same concepts. The distinguishing feature of asset management, however, is its central focus on assets, their condition, and their performance. Systems such as ERP are based on costs and, in particular, on manpower costs versus manpower performance and progress toward selected goals. Asset management optimizes, rather, on asset performance versus cost and is more suited to transportation organizations with substantial investments in physical assets.

There has been some confusion about the relationship between management systems and asset management. Management systems provide key information and analysis capabilities to agencies implementing asset management principles, but they do not constitute the whole of asset management. Decisions rendered in an asset management environment are much broader in scope, require substantially more economic analysis, and normally involve more than one kind of asset. Transportation Asset Management focuses on the whole transportation infrastructure, and makes possible decisions that reflect the optimal performance of that infrastructure compared to the resources required to operate and maintain it. Additionally, asset management examines investment timing, tools, and economic analyses to assure the effective use of available funds. For example, if borrowing rates are high, an economic analysis might look at tradeoffs between increased costs of repairs due to delaying the work and additional costs incurred by borrowing funds at the current, higher interest rate. Another example is evaluating the overall benefit-cost advantages of conducting regular pavement preservation efforts as compared to resurfacing and replacement. Yet another example is examining tradeoffs between construction costs and maintenance costs over the life of the asset (such as cost savings from installing median guardrail over turf versus maintenance costs for the turf over many years).

What Transportation Asset Management Means to the Public Agency

Those who work in transportation have in common three primary goals:

Keeping the infrastructure in as good or better condition than it is now.

Developing and implementing a logical capital improvement plan.

Containing the costs of planning, building, operating, and maintaining the facilities.

Transportation Asset Management is focused on the transportation infrastructure, and its use directly impacts these three goals. The emphasis on "more information on which to base decisions" leads to higher accountability for officials charged with making those decisions and, to some extent, a new way of looking at managing transportation infrastructure. Programs have to be directed toward defined performance goals and either show solid return on investment or face changes-similar to the way in which private industry focuses on market share and rate of return.

Transportation systems continue to grow rapidly and become increasingly complex. Asset management provides new insights and tools to help transportation professionals make wise investments that result in improved service and greater cost-effectiveness. Because information is central to effective implementation of asset management, each agency has to determine how much information is enough, and that will depend on its goals and its willingness to take risks. It is not cost-effective-or even possible-to have 100 percent assurance for every decision; determining the balance between assurance and cost is one of the key considerations for any asset management program.

Know future needs – decision support processes and demand

Demand management

Providing LoS in the most cost effective manner to present and future customers requires forecasting of both what the required LoS might be and how many customers may be requiring these services.

These two unknowns (future LoS and future customer numbers) are collectively known as “demand”.

Demand can be for increased or decreased services (e.g. we no longer need road-side water troughs for horses). Demand for new or increased services or for increased numbers to use an existing service does not necessarily have to be met; it can be ”managed down” even to the point of elimination through provision of alternatives, disincentives and other demand management techniques.

Demand management (which is a non-asset solution) is

active intervention in the market to influence demand for services and assets, with forecast consequences. The objective of demand management is to influence the demand for services and assets to avoid or defer asset investment by:

Altering customers' expectations of the service they will receive

Optimising asset utilisation/performance

Reducing demand for new/replaced assets

Involving consumers in determining selected services and standards

Separating proven needs from expectations.

Successful demand management should increase economic and social benefits to the community. Historically, service providers have attempted, with varying degrees of success, to meet demand for services without questioning or attempting to modify demand. This approach tends to raise customer expectations and invariably leads to even further demand. Increasing focus on strategic planning, fiscal responsibility, user pays, and core service reviews has created greater awareness of the need to consider demand management.

Demand management may be considered as having up to four major components, with each of these having a number of implementation options:

Demand Substitution – provide alternatives such as incentives pricing structures, metered use and subsidies, for instance

Restrictions – restrict type of use, time of use and methodology

Education – change habits, increase understanding, and promote alternatives.

Maintenance management

Maintenance can be defined as "all actions necessary for retaining an asset as near as practical to its original condition, but excluding rehabilitation or renewal." It is important to remember that some assets will and should fail.

There are two major categories of maintenance:

Planned (proactive) – work that delays or prevents a known failure mode, e.g. the painting of bridge beams will delay the onset of rusting and possible structural failure

Reactive Maintenance Cost

Proactive Maintenance Cost

Total Maintenance Cost

Optimal Zone

Unplanned (Reactive) – when a fault is identified and is fixed but is not part of the planned maintenance programme e.g. a dangerous pothole is identified and filled.

Figure: Relationships between maintenance planning costs and work costs.

Degree of Planning

This figure highlights the need to balance the amount of reactive and planned maintenance work. Relying on reactive maintenance only would result in higher total costs. The task of the maintenance manager is to achieve the right mix so that total costs lie in the optimal band.

Some practices that help to manage maintenance

effectively include those listed below.

maintenance engineering analysis, which is a process of logical evaluation to determine the maintenance needs relevant to the operating environment and the organisation's objectives. A reliability-centred maintenance approach provides the optimal blend of planned and unplanned maintenance, especially for critical assets. In this process, the following questions are addressed:
What is the asset's required function?
How does it fail?
What causes it to fail?
What happens when it fails?
What can be done to prevent failure?
What action is required if failure cannot be prevented?
Pavement maintenance management Systems These build on analysis performed to identify those items or assets that display specific or likely failure modes but generally do not identify all possible failures for all items. Because of their roles in meeting objectives or a defined level of facility function, these systems can be very worthwhile, but pre-adoption analysis should be subject to the same Optimized Decision-Making routines as other asset management decisions.
The outputs from the TSA are lists of road sections (treatment lengths) with an indication of the road maintenance treatments required on each section, with the financial costs and user benefits of carrying out the pavement maintenance treatment indicated. These are calculated from the condition of the sections recorded in RAMM during the condition evaluation inspections.
The TSA allows you to set a financial performance level in

terms of Benefit:Cost (B:C) ratio, above which a shape correction treatment is selected. The B:C ratio represents the ratio of benefits (i.e. road user benefits obtained from roughness reduction) to construction costs (i.e. the shape correction treatment cost less maintenance savings). If all the shape correction treatments selected were actioned by the RCA this would limit the roughness of all roads in the network categorized by traffic volume. The B:C ratio chosen is therefore also a de-facto functional performance level for the road network.

The TSA applies user input maintenance and renewal costs and produces reasonably accurate results in the short term (one to three years). It is not as accurate over longer periods and does not consider unsealed roads at all.

maintenance intervention Strategies (miS) A MIS is a detailed statement of the type of maintenance activity that should be targeted to the treatment lengths identified in the forward work programme (FWP). It is the principal method of conveying the appropriate maintenance activities to all parties involved in the maintenance of an asset. A MIS can be developed for any asset class.

MIS are designed to ensure the optimum use of maintenance funding by ensuring that routine activities are appropriate, given the programmed treatments.

maintenance intervention exceptions These are a sub-set of full intervention strategies. They are used by some authorities to document exceptions to normal maintenance practices, such as pothole repairs before overlays, without developing a full MIS. They should be regarded as the first step on the road to MIS development and not an end-point in themselves. Like MIS, Maintenance Intervention Exceptions can be developed for any asset class.

Renewal management

Pavement renewals in the short term can be forecast using RAMM, TSA or dTIMS. The best forecaster of pavement renewals beyond three years is dTIMS. However, it may not be an economically viable tool on lightly trafficked networks, because the costs of collecting and analysing the data on roads with Annual Average Daily Traffic (AADT) counts of below about 500 vehicles/day may not be balanced by the greater precision and certainty dTIMS can provide when compared with other techniques. The use of dTIMS should be subject to an Optimized Decision Making (ODM) process.

Although dTIMS can be used to model longer periods, its default setups are for 20 years, which is shorter than the lifecycle of all but the busiest pavements. Renewal requirements for longer periods can be modelled in dTIMS by "banding" years (e.g. in threes to coincide with the Long Term Plan Cycle).

Another technique for estimating long term renewal needs for pavements and all other roading assets is to use a soundly based asset valuation, ideally a condition based one, to establish the base- year's need, then aging and renewing the assets using spread sheet techniques to forecast annual renewals. While it is generally not a suitable tool for network level investigation or justification of projects, Net Present Value (NPV) analysis and its sibling, B:C ratio analysis (BCR) can be very useful at the option section stage of projects. NZTAs Project Evaluation Manual should be used as the basis for this work.

Before embarking on any renewal project, the need for the renewal should be tested against the required LoS and justified by the asset failure risk.

Management of improvements and new work needs

New works and improvements can only be properly justified by referral to the required LoS. However, LoS can often be affected by projected changes to other assets or services outside the roadway. For example, a new university would generate needs for new facilities across the whole nearby road network.

Understanding what could go wrong – risk management and critical assets

Knowing and understanding the risks faced by assets and the organisation facilitates the management of those risks in ways that help produce and maintain the desired LoS for present and future customers at the lowest lifecycle cost.

Infrastructure risk management is the process of identifying risks that may affect the assets' on- going service delivery. Risk management is often considered a core activity that influences the way the principal asset-based activities (creation, maintenance, renewal and disposal) are carried out. For this reason, although section 4.2.6 of the IIMM 2011 suggests risk be considered in the AMPs Lifecycle Management section, many RCAs consider it separately, along with growth and other asset drivers, before they detail their lifecycle management plans.

A consistent risk management framework should be applied within each organisation, across all its sectors or divisions so risks can be compared and addressed appropriately. Recommended processes for risk identification and evaluation are described in the RIMS manual, along with suggested risk frameworks and registers.

The risk analysis output should be a table of the asset-based risks faced by the organization.

An AMP should discuss risk. Good practice is for:

Risks to be incorporated into the AMPs considerations and processes

Outcomes from the risk management process to be integrated throughout the AMP and reflected in its maintenance, renewal and improvement programmes

Any innovations linking the risk management framework and other organisational systems to be included in the AM Improvement Plan and implemented as appropriate.

Identification of critical assets

Identifying critical assets and vulnerabilities is an important step to understanding and improving resilience to adverse events.

Critical assets are usually defined as those that have high consequences of failure, even though there may not be very high probabilities of this occurring. Similarly, the critical failure modes of an asset are those with the highest consequences of failure. Bridges over major rivers are often critical assets because there are few alternative routes and these usually require a long deviation. For example; there are only two bridges over the Rakaia River; if the SH1 Bridge fails, the eight-km drive between Rakaia and Bankside becomes a 102-km journey.

Critical risks should be noted or differentiated clearly in the risk table. They will often be extracted from the table and given special consideration in the risk reduction strategy or plan.

Risk treatment

As the purpose of risk evaluation is to allow risk to be

managed, treatments or actions to address the risks after must also to be considered. The following treatment matrix can be used for this purpose. The organization's risk management policy should contain information that provides similar guidance to this.

Low consequence–high likelihood risks can often be managed though maintenance contracts
High consequence–high likelihood events need to be prioritised for more detailed analysis and intervention
High consequence–low likelihood events need to be evaluated; although they may be unlikely to occur, they have a high impact when they do occur
Low consequence–low likelihood events will generally be monitored.
Risk can be managed using one or a combination of the following options:
Accepting the risk
Reducing the likelihood of a failure
Reducing the consequences of a failure.
Individual risk reduction interventions can be asset related or non-asset related. The following figure outlines these.

Risk prioritisation
There are likely to be a large number of identified risks. As they will almost never be able to be addressed at the same time it is necessary to priorities the interventions. Risk reduction options for individual assets, within specific asset classes (such as bridges or roads) within an activity (e.g. transportation/roading) and within the organization can be managed using the same techniques as other AM decisions. These include b:c analyses and multi-criteria

analyses.

Some people believe prioritizing risk interventions should be based on the risk score (i.e. the higher the risk scores, the higher the priority). This may not be best way to priorities risks. For example,

a natural disaster risk may have the highest score, but any amount of proposed action may not appreciably affect the total risk of the event. A more appropriate method of prioritizing asset-risk interventions may be to consider the reductions in risk that would be achieved by the proposed interventions and rank them accordingly.

The NZTA Deficiency Database and Prioritization Process (DDPP)4 contains a risk-based prioritization process.

Further information on project evaluation and prioritization is contained in the IIMM and the RIMs, "Best-practice Guidelines".

Outputs from risk analysis process

Sound and effective risk analysis should produce the following outputs or inform the following processes:

Prioritised lists of asset improvements/alterations and new works required to reduce risk exposure, plus the works' estimated costs

Changes to current practices to reduce risk exposure

Asset maintenance procedures, priorities and practices

Asset renewal priorities and standards

Asset development (new work and improvement) strategies, priorities and standards

Details of accepted or acceptable risks

Asset disposal priorities, standards and practices.

Know future needs – financial forecasts

Financial linkages

Well researched and soundly based maintenance, renewal, improvement and disposal plans that will provide the required LoS at the lowest lifecycle costs for current and future customers are virtually useless unless they are funded. In an agency with mature AM practices fully integrated into its organizational systems and processes, budgets will usually be set on the basis of the AM needs developed through the AM process. At less developed levels of maturity, budgets will often be set with varying degrees of relationship to the assets' needs, or their ability to deliver specified LoS. However, even in agencies exhibiting the highest levels of AM maturity there will be occasions when the assets' immediate needs cannot be met by available funding.

The relationships between the AMP and its annual, medium and long term financial forecasts will ideally be straight forward and direct, with the budgets, financial plans and forecasts repeating the information in the AMP.

Figure : The budgeting continuum.

The ideal case shown in Figure 2.8-1 above is not achievable in practice because the influences affecting the annual budgets and financial forecasts cover many things that are beyond an AMPs compass. Therefore, annual plans and financial forecasts that do not meet the assets' full needs will often be proposed and be given effect. In reality, resource allocation and budgeting are components of the continuum illustrated in Figure 2.8 2 below. Changing any part of this continuum will affect all the other parts.

This continuum shows resource allocation is immediately affected by a change in budget. A change in budget influences LoS, and the asset's expected end-of-period condition and performance. A change in budget will affect the agency's performance. Section 3.5.6 of the IIMM includes a subsection on dealing with financial constraints.

These considerations provide the basis for appropriate AM recognition of a reduced or increased budget. The appropriate response is to:

Review planned resource allocations

Determine the effects these will have on agreed LoS

Assess how these changes in LoS will be reflected in the end of period asset condition and performance

Adjust the work plan as necessary to achieve the best possible life cycle asset condition and performance within the available budget (this may mean leaving some assets' condition to decline to the extent that they require more expensive actions later)

Assess the effects of the revised programmes on the agency's performance targets

Report the anticipated effects on the targets to senior management.

Long term assessments of the asset's financial needs and funding requirements are crucial outputs from AMP, and their associated financial management practices.

These forecasts should bring together all relevant data from all AM processes

They should be underpinned by clearly articulated assumptions and confidence factors

The forecast period for local authorities must be at least ten years. Local authorities are also required to forecast the first three years "in detail".

The main elements of financial forecasts should:

IncludeNew works and improvements, sometimes called development

Maintenance and operations

Renewals

Disposals

Forecast future depreciation needs and changes in network service potential

Forecast for a significant period, at least 10 years

Include the financial outcomes of the AM strategies and programmes derived in the AMP

Be based on provable data, recorded key assumptions and have defined confidence levels

Be updated annually.

Inflation

The Audit Office has advised local authorities that their financial forecasts must include the effects of forecast inflation. However, this is unhelpful from an AM view as the effects of inflation are usually greater than any other influences on asset budgets, and thus can mask or hide useful AM information.

The most practical means of addressing this dilemma is to:

Prepare all estimates and forecasts in the AMP on a no inflation basis

Detail the forecast inflation in a separate sub-section of the AMP dedicated to financial forecasts

Assemble the financial information that is to go forward to the financial forecasts/budget approval process in "constant dollar" and "including inflation" forms.

The NZ Society of Local Government Managers (SOLGM) commissions an independent forecast of expected inflation annually.

Examples of financial forecasts on these bases are shown below. It can be seen that although the forecast without inflation (constant-dollar forecast) shows costs to be almost constant in real terms, rising only 3.7 % in 10-years the forecast including inflation gives an impression of costs rising by 41%.

Figure: Comparison of financial forecasts.

Forecasting approach

Financial forecasts can be prepared and presented using either straightforward or complex approaches. It is helpful to consider the results required which will invariably be required to be clear and straightforward.

Clear and straightforward forecasts can be prepared in detail or at any desired macro level. However, while it can be relatively quick and simple to produce a macro-level estimate, to do so with any degree of accuracy usually requires a degree of hidden complexity and hidden assumptions. These forecasts can become complex to use when it becomes necessary to make changes during the budgeting process and the assumptions and linkages between items are not apparent or established.

When preparing financial forecasts and estimates, it is often simpler to prepare them to one level of detail below the lowest used in the financial system. While this may initially appear complex, the additional certainty and changeability of the data, together with the ability to record specific assumptions and projects and trace different aspects of the same project (e.g. income and expenditure or "subsidised" and "unsubsidised" renewals) often makes this approach simpler to use in the long term and easier to follow when the forecasts are revisited. The renewals' summaries illustrated above appear very simple and straightforward. They are the results of the summation of forecasts prepared this way.

Data presentation is another important aspect of the forecasting approach. Financial staff will obviously need detailed numbers. However, many users, including AM staff, can often get more information from a chart than a table. The ability to combine both charts and tables, as is done in the example above, provides an effective solution for most potential users.

Know what you don't know – asset management improvement

Plan or Continuous Improvement Plan, but a less confusing name is the AM Improvement Section.

AM Improvement must not be confused with an Asset Improvement Plan (i.e. new works, development and asset improvements). This is a common confusion and the reason behind the suggested name for this section.

The principal output of the AM Improvement Section is an improvement plan that identifies the resources required to enhance existing elements of the business, or to implement new elements to deliver the longer-term strategic goals and objectives of the organization. The AM Improvement

Plan should priorities the steps or tasks, allocate resources to them and programme them. A typical improvement plan is developed through the following steps or processes:

Identify corporate needs for AM planning

Assess the current status of the AM practices
Evaluate the gaps between current and desired needs and practices
Develop an optimised improvement programme to close those gaps, considering options, risks, costs and availability of resources
Specify AMP improvement outcomes for each task and allocate responsibilities and resources
Include a system for continuous review and monitoring of the AMP's effectiveness.
The AM Improvement section of the AMP should summarise current and assess future AM practices, providing an understanding of how AM decisions are made and how AM practices will be improved.
It should also provide details on monitoring the AMPs performance and any improvements to AM systems that will improve the level of confidence in the AMP.

Linking Stages and Implementation
16.a. Linking Strategic levels with operational levels

One of the principles behind sound infrastructure AM is that the links between works that are carried out on individual assets and the organisation's highest level goals and objectives should be very clear and appropriately understood by all those involved in maintaining, procuring or providing the assets.
We have seen that the objective of infrastructural AM is to provide the desired LoS in the most cost effective manner for present and future customers, and that achieving this objective requires an understanding of LoS.
LoS are the link between an organization's vision and its

tactical and operational plans and thus to activities "on the road". Figure 3.1 1 illustrates the position of LoS. They sit between high-level corporate objectives and the more detailed operational plans and procedures.
Figure 16.a. : Linking works and operations with the corporate vision.

The vision and high level corporate objectives or strategic outcomes are often stated in relatively vague terms, for example:
Safe roads
A resilient and secure transport network
Easing of severe urban congestion
Reductions in deaths and serious injuries from road crashes.
As we move down through the 'hierarchy of documents and procedures outlined in Figure 3.1 1 we become much more specific about what is to be done to achieve these goals. The corporate vision could be "Safe Roads", for example.
Figure 3.1 2: Works and operations activities linked to the corporate vision.

16.b. Linking different planning stage
One person is unlikely to be responsible for all aspects of a network's maintenance, operation, renewal, development, AM and project management. People at different levels within an organisation may be jointly involved with similar stages. Bringing these different levels together may be difficult, or in some cases one level may overshadow another. It is therefore necessary to design and implement processes that collect all the appropriate inputs, resolve

differences and any conflicts, and then produce sound, effective and widely supported plans and programmes that will provide the agreed LoS to present and future customers for the lowest lifecycle costs.

The parties involved in this planning may not all be direct employees of the organisation that owns the assets. The discussions on maintenance, operations and renewals should involve selected staff from the maintenance contractors who can contribute to the discussions, help optimise and co- ordinate programmes, and contribute to discussions on better ways of doing things and removing impediments or bottlenecks. There is also a strong likelihood that internal supervisory staff and contractors will be able to provide useful feedback and suggestions for standards of new works and improvements and difficulties or problems encountered with recent new works. This latter point is particularly relevant in areas subject to growth where new subdivision roads are designed and built by developers.

The Figure below illustrates linkages between the different asset activities or stages of an assets lifecycle that need to be considered at all times. They are explained further below.

Figure: Linkages between asset activities.

While some of these linkages will require immediate or prompt recognition, others require longer- term recognition. For example, reflection of the future reseal needs of a new road in the renewals budget maybe seven or more years in the future. This is not a valid reason to ignore them; rather, it is a good reason to extend the forecasting period. However, extension beyond 20-years is likely to be only of academic interest unless very long term forecasting is being done.

16.b.i. New works and improvements links

links with maintenance And operations

The greatest influence on the lifecycle costs of infrastructural assets occurs in the asset creation stage. This is not simply because of the cost of construction but because of the influences and effects that the location, design, materials and construction standards will have on the frequency, cost and levels of maintenance and renewals required throughout its life.

The links described below must be made:

Maintenance and operations budgets and budget forecasts must reflect known and planned additions to the network. It is easy to dismiss additional maintenance cost and operational costs; for example, inspections and cleaning costs for one kilometre of new street or a new bridge. However, the effects of all such works are obviously cumulative, and failure to recognise the effects of individual changes will usually have two adverse effects on the network:

The budget available for maintenance and operations will be effectively reduced on a per km or per unit basis. Forcing more to be done with less is not viable when optimal maintenance systems have been developed, as such changes are by definition sub-optimal or less economic in the long term

The time will come when it is necessary to increase the budgets, because they will be obviously inadequate to maintain desired standards. These increases are also likely to be large, controversial and financially painful.

Maintenance and operations contracts for all the asset elements must be altered to include the new or altered assets

Construction standards and designs for new works and improvements must reflect the need to provide LoS at the lowest lifecycle costs. This can be a particular issue in new subdivisions as there is incentive for the developers to produce "window dressing" enhancements that have high lifecycle costs and avoid hidden works that will reduce those costs. Some examples are:

Extensive use of interlocking concrete blocks and asphaltic concrete as carriageway surfaces but resistance to construction of adequate base and sub-base layers

Use of expensive, unique streetlight poles and fittings, to provide a "marketing edge" with no thought to maintenance, replacement of damaged poles in-service life and need for eventual renewal

Erection of ornamental walls, often with "fancy" signage, on what will become road reserve, also to provide a "marketing edge". These walls and the attached signage usually become maintenance liabilities for the ultimate road owner, do not deliver any agreed LoS, can increase the likelihood of injury in traffic crashes and become difficult for the RCA to remove because residents value them.

links with renewals And rehabilitation

The linkages between new works, and renewals and rehabilitation needs are twofold:

Budgetary, but on longer timeframes and for higher individual amounts than the maintenance effects

Programme related, as it is often more economical for some asset improvements to be carried out at the same time as renewal works or just ahead of them, e.g. sealed widening, in conjunction with a pavement renewal. Establishing the most appropriate timeframe and scheduling requires consideration of lifecycle costs and design options. Similarly it may be appropriate to delay a planned renewal, such as a resurfacing, until after a planned new work has occurred.

links with non-roading works

New works can influence non-roading assets because so many of them are located in the road reserve, including under the carriageway. While the influences run both ways, as indicated in Figure, the responsibility for carrying out the co-ordination lies fully on the party proposing the work; e.g. a major road realignment and new bridge may require co-ordination with operators of the following utilities:

Water supply

Sewerage

Stormwater

Reticulated gas

Electricity

Telecommunications

Railways.

links with disposals

If the new work is not to be a permanent feature of the network then its disposal should be included in forward programmes. Its disposal cost should also be included in the consideration of the project's lifecycle costs and economic viability.

Disposals also need to be considered when construction of a new asset removes the need for the services provided by an existing asset in a different location e.g. a road realignment may remove the need for a bridge and its approaches.

Disposal costs must be fully programmed, either as part of the construction project's cost or separately. Disposal costs include:

Consultation

Removing the asset that is no longer required

The costs of preparation for sale, such as surveying, fencing or conversion to another use

Costs of sale

Making the site safe after the asset has been removed.

Disposal income should similarly be programmed. It is good practice to programme the income and expenditure associated with each disposal as separate budget items, although they will usually be summed to give a net result. Separate programming ensures all the steps needed to safely dispose of the redundant asset are fully considered and provided for.

16.b.ii. Maintenance and operations links

Although maintenance and operations practices should influence the standards and specifications for new works and improvements, there are no major effects that maintenance and operations decisions should have on new works programmes.

Similarly, there are no significant links required between maintenance programmes and disposal programmes. Those links run the other way with maintenance programmes reflecting decisions to dispose of assets. The influence of inadequate maintenance on the life and eventual disposal of assets is indirect, through renewal and rehabilitation.

16.b.iii. links with renewals and rehabilitation

Sub-optimal maintenance practices can adversely affect the service lives of road components, thus requiring more frequent renewals. However, unless there is a deliberate decision made to reduce maintenance on an asset and the effects of the reduction can be reliably estimated at the time, the renewal programming and budgeting link is usually indirect. The more significant effect is from the operations side of this activity.

Operations affect renewal and rehabilitation works through the results of the inspections and condition measurement. Failure to programme or fund levels of inspection and asset monitoring appropriate to each asset element will result in less efficient and effective renewal and rehabilitation programmes. This may force abandonment of some programmed renewals, and consequent increases in costs and reductions in levels of service, so reactive works can be carried out to respond to unpredicted failures.

Renewals and rehabilitation links

links with new works And improvements

The need to carry out renewals can influence the timing of improvements and renewals. The New Works and Improvements programme and the Renewal and Rehabilitation programmes require careful co-ordination to ensure optimal decisions are made.

links with non-roading works And other roading renewal Programmes

In roading authorities where only one or two people are

involved in all the renewal decisions it is relatively simple to co-ordinate the renewal of different roading assets. However, in larger authorities this is not so straightforward and particular attention is required to ensure that the right works

are done at the right time, in the right order, so lifecycle costs can be reduced, and disruption of customers minimised. The need to co-ordinate renewal programmes for the different segments of the road renewal programme is really no different from the need to co-ordinate with other utility operators.

An example requiring such co-ordination, which also includes non-roading assets, is reconstruction of streets in residential areas. In many cases all the services in these streets were all installed about the same time, and although many have different lifecycles, eventually there are a number of major elements that will need renewing over a relatively short period, of say 10 to 15 years. Other assets that are further removed from the ends of their lives may also be present but, in terms of the overall cost effectiveness of combining works, it may be better to curtail their lives and replace them early as part of a major reconstruction project. In this way the need to replace the sewer, pavement or kerb and channel can drive rebuild of a street that renews:

Berms

Footpaths

Kerbs and channels

Water supply sub-mains

Water supply mains

Sewers

Electrical reticulation

Street lighting
Gas reticulation
Pavement layers
Pavement surface
Telecommunications cables and facilities including on-street cell-phone towers.
Disposals links
There are no significant direct links between disposals and new works; the link is in the reverse direction.

links with maintenance And operations
When an asset disposal is planned the maintenance needs of that asset should reduce to the minimum level to adequately provide the required levels of service, including safety, for the balance of the assets life. If the disposal date is some years away, amendment to the Maintenance Intervention Strategy or Maintenance Intervention Exceptions List are usually appropriate
The maintenance and operations programmes, contracts and associated systems must also be adjusted to reflect the reduction in the asset base caused by the disposal. Budgets may be adjusted but, as disposals are rare, there is little danger of cumulative effects causing later problems if this is not done. The decision to immediately reflect the disposal in maintenance and operations budget and programme forecasts will depend on the significance of the disposal.

links with renewals And rehabilitation
The effects and responses for renewals are likely to be similar to those affecting maintenance and operations. It is necessary to review all FWPs to ensure aspects or elements

of the disposed asset are not included in forecast renewals.

links with non-roading works

The same principles apply here as have already been canvassed in previous sub-sections of 3.2.

In some cases the needs of other utility operators may prevent the demolition of an asset or its sale to a third party, instead requiring disposal to the utility operator so it can continue to meet that utility's needs.

Non-roading works

The Utilities Access Act 2010 requires non-roading utilities to be consulted over works that affect or may affect them. It is also in the RCA's interest to consult these organizations, as failure to do so may result in work that reduces the road assets' effective useful life. For example, a reconstructed footpath could be dug up a year or two later to renew a water main.

The National Code of Practice for Utility Operators' Access to Transport Corridors (November 20115) is a statutory means of compliance with the Act.

16.c. Funding and Planning

Funding is different from financial forecasts and budgets, although approved budgets are often described as "approved funding". In this context funding is consideration of where the finance to meet the financial forecasts will come from.

Funding pressures and shocks to finance infrastructure investment have historically arisen through a combination of factors:

Lack of basic information on past performance and asset condition inhibiting prediction of future asset performance and asset failures

Lack of detailed information on the past costs of maintaining and renewing assets, such as analysis of maintenance sub categories
No robust assessment of maintenance or renewal gaps
Assets valued at historic cost – because there is no revaluation regime – so consumption of assets (depreciation) is either not considered or it is understated
Short-term budgets that do not signal long-term funding issues
Budgets based on cash forecasts and cash availability rather than being not accrual based
Ignoring the effects of increased asset stock on operating and maintenance forecasts
Funding allocated to new projects to the detriment of maintaining and renewing the existing asset stock
Lack of transparency in consulting with potential funders and lack of transparency in the disclosure of likely funding amounts
Reluctance by decision makers to face funding issues.

To reduce the likelihoods of these events occurring and their severities the financial manager and the asset manager need to project future revenue or funding sources and cash flows alongside the financial forecast. Note that this is a combined effort, not the sole responsibility of the asset manager. For New Zealand Local Authorities, the two principal sources of funding for roading are rates and NZTA financial assistance, often incorrectly called "subsidy". The processes for NZTA financial assistance and calculation of expected levels of financial assistance are detailed in its Planning Programme and Funding Manual.

In broad terms, in any local government operation, rates

must fund all expenses that are not met from other sources which, in addition to NZTA financial assistance, include:

Development Contributions received to facilitate works to offset the immediate effects of land development levied under the Local Government Act 2002

Financial Contributions received to facilitate works to offset the wider effects of significant land development on the road network and levied under the Resource Management Act

Fees and charges

Borrowing.

Although projection of future funding needs is the joint duty of asset managers and financial planners, in practice, the roading asset manager will usually be required to forecast:

NZTA Financial assistance receipts

Income from Financial Contributions that is being used to meet some of the costs of the development work detailed in the relevant resource consents

Income from Development Contributions being used to meet some of the costs of the network development work detailed in the relevant resource consents.

The budgeting continuum in Section 2.8.1 describes the linkages between funding (budgets), asset condition, budgets and LoS.

16.c.i. Forecasting NZTA Financial Assistance

NZTA advises all local authorities of the financial assistance rates at which it will support their road maintenance, renewal and improvement works. The Agency has also adopted a practice of capping the total amount of financial assistance it will provide in each year of a three-year cycle; this is tied to Treasury forecasting cycles. The net effect of this cap is that financial assistance rates will differ from the published percentage figures, especially in years two and three of the forecasts as inflation affects "subsidisable" costs but not the financial assistance cap.

The net effect of these two factors is that the asset manager should:

Develop the forecast financial assistance income on a line-by-line basis, relating each element of the forecast to a specific group of financially assisted works

Cap the calculated financial assistance at the advised amount for the three years it has been determined by the NZTA

Forecast the full value of financial assistance, at current agreed rates, for the balance of the forecast period.

16.c.ii. Forecasting financial and development-contribution incomes

The laws, case-law and regulations around Financial Contributions and Development contributions are restrictive. Their net effect is, in summary, that the finance collected may only be used for the purposes detailed in the consents and the resulting works must be completed within specified time frames. As these moneys are usually held by local authorities in trust accounts or similar until they are required, the total amounts currently available can be ascertained relatively simply. The total amounts of Financial Contributions due are detailed in the individual Resource Consents and in the case of Development Contributions, in the detail of the Council resolutions authorising them.

The asset manager should include the income associated with each financial contribution work and each development contribution work in the financial forecasts. It is good practice to identify each work and each income line separately so that the elements of each work can be related, and any changes are simplified.

16.c.iii. Forecasting income from fees and charges

The most common fee or charge that is likely to be encountered in this context is Corridor Access and Road Opening fees, although there are many authorities that do not charge for these. The way income from fees and charges is handled in the financial and funding forecasts will depend on the organisation's policies; whether they are used to directly offset the costs of managing and supervising the road openings or whether they are part of "general income" which is used to offset total expenditure. Another likely source of income is outdoor parking, where this is under the jurisdiction of the roading unit.

Regardless of how the organisation treats income, it remains good practice to separately forecast the costs and incomes associated with each area for which fees and charges are received.

16.c.iv. Forecasting loans

This area is best left to the financial staff. If asked to do such forecasts the asset manager should immediately seek advice and assistance from them.

16.c.v. Other aspects of planning funding of roading activities

All roading authorities will have financial, forecasting and consultation policies and possibly by-laws that address:

Sustainability

Intergenerational equity

Transparency

Fairness

Defensibility
Consultation and engagement with iwi, other communities, community groups, key stakeholders and other interested parties and government agencies
Risk and uncertainty
Value for money.
These policies should be read, understood, followed, and be incorporated as appropriate into asset management practices.

developing An Asset management Plan

The AMP is a described in the IIMM as an "Asset Management enabler". This is an appropriate and accurate description. AMPs) are not an end in themselves; they are developed to facilitate the goal of AM:

» The provision of the required LoS to present and future customers in the most cost effective manner.

This objective and these Road Transportation Asset Management Guidelines emphasise the paramount position of LoS. They are the keys to the successful development and implementation of good AM practices and AMPs. They are also the foundation upon which all recommendations, conclusions, decisions and budgets developed in the AMP should be based.

AMPs are not necessarily one document; they may span several volumes or can even occupy entire bookcases. Their essential feature is that they establish what, when, why and how assets are to be acquired, maintained, renewed and disposed of to provide the required LoS and the expected costs to current and future customers.

Plan For Plan revision

An AMP should be written keeping in mind the need to

change it frequently to reflect the above changes. Adopting a structure, document formatting and writing practices that will simplify updating will return significant benefits.

One example of this is providing source information with all charts and tables that are prepared in other documents such as spread sheets. This can be done with a formula that returns text such as that below.

Another good practice is to structure the plan so that it does not need to be rewritten in its entirety whenever changes are necessary to a specific section or sections. However, it is rare that changes to one part of the AMP will not affect parts of the Lifecycle Management Plan, financial plan and the executive summary. This is one reason for splitting the Lifecycle Management Plan into discrete sections covering each element of the lifecycle (maintenance, renewal etc.) and risk. It is also beneficial to have the Financial Plan as a stand-alone section so that annual changes to inflation forecasts can be easily incorporated.

17.a. identifying expected outputs And outcomes

The high and intermediate level outcomes of sound AM planning are listed in Section 1.4. These outcomes lead to the following expected outputs and outcomes of AMPs.

17.a.i. Organisational recognition

The AMP is approved and adopted by the governing body, board or council. This includes their approval of the AM Improvement section of the plan.

The AMP is the key planning tool for its assets and is the sole source of asset information for organisation's strategic plans/LTP

AMPs are up to date and reflect the current demands on

and needs for the assets they cover

AMPs are implemented through operational plans, and discrepancies are formally reported

Financial programmes, budgets and forecasts will reflect the forecasts developed in AMPs and adopted by the organisation

Budget changes required by financial constraints or required to meet unanticipated new requirements will be worked through the AM planning process before adoption, so future maintenance and renewal implications and the full effects on present and proposed LoS can be considered.

17.a.ii. Levels of service

LoS required of the asset are clearly linked to the strategic/community outcomes of the organisation

Customer LoS are understood at Board/Council level, by all members of the executive management team and by customers and are supported by technical LoS

Customer LoS are adopted at Board/Council level after:

Evaluating of LoS options

Undertaking consultation on LoS options with the community and other relevant stakeholders (using consultation processes which meet industry recognised standards)

Customer LoS and standards are promulgated in a 'Customer Charter' or equivalent public document

LoS for significant aspects of the roading/transportation are detailed in the organisations LTP and AMPs

The AMPs of each significant service reflect and are based on the agreed LoS, including technical performance measures which underpin the customer agreed LoS and standards

Technical LoS are soundly based and understood by all practitioners, designers, maintainers, contractors and others working on the network

LoS are SMART

Achievement or otherwise of LoS is:

Gauged through use of SMART performance and condition measures, key performance indicators (KPIs) and key performance measures (KPMs) that are evaluated and reassessed regularly and often; i.e. performance and condition measures, KPIs and KPMs are SMARTER

Reported to the public at regular fixed intervals, at least annually.

17.a.iii. Asset knowledge

There is a reliable physical inventory of assets at both an individual asset level and at a network level, including:

Physical attributes such as location, material and age

Systematic monitoring and analysis of physical condition

Systematic measurement of asset performance (including utilisation/capacity)

The remaining useful lives of assets.

The assets' financial description is linked to the physical description, with the ability to aggregate and disaggregate information, and meet the requirements of:

Financial Reporting Standards

Valuation Standards augmented by the NZ Depreciation and Valuation Guidelines.

17.a.iv. Growth management (positive or negative)

Gaps between current service capacities/capabilities and those required to meet current and future LoS are understood and documented

Demand forecasts for each network/facility are based on the latest growth forecasts and at least cover a 10-year period

Demand forecasts include analysis of the different factors that comprise demand

The sensitivities of asset development (new works) programmes to demand changes are understood

There is clear differentiation between the need for works to provide for growth and those required to provide for changes LoS.

17.a.v. Risk management

Critical assets and associated risks are identified and risk management strategies developed using risk management principals and techniques.

AM decisions always recognise and apply the principles of integrated risk management; specifically:

Risk management practices are aligned with ISO 31000 (formerly AS/NZS 4360), and industry good practice such as the NZ Local Government Handbook for risk management

Asset risk management is integrated with other corporate risk management processes

Asset risk management encompasses:

Identifying risk management strategies for all critical assets

Risk assessments and mitigation plans for engineering lifelines/lifeline utilities, which will include reference to the organisation's disaster recovery and business continuity plans

Establishing links to asset maintenance and replacement strategies.

17.a.vi. Optimised decision-making

Optimised Decision-Making techniques (ODM) are used throughout all lifecycle management process and to develop solutions to fill these gaps using an asset development and/or disposal programmes

ODM is the basis of robust and defensible options for asset treatments and developments that achieve optimal costs over their life cycles and the network's lifecycle, including:

Applying appropriate economic evaluation tools (or other organisation endorsed prioritisation systems) in developing short-term project lists

Using predictive modelling techniques to provide defensible long-term financial forecasts

Evaluation and ranking of options for significant capital investment decisions is based on suitable criteria.

17.a.vii. Financial forecasts

AM Planning translates the physical aspects of planned maintenance, renewal and new work into financial terms for at least the ensuing 10 years and in a manner that is fair, consistent and transparent.

The forecasts include sufficient information to enable decline in service potential (depreciation) of an asset to be measured. (Guidance on depreciation is included in the NZ Valuation and Depreciation Guidelines.)

AM Planning translates the physical aspects of planned operational, maintenance, renewal, new and disposal works into financial terms generally over the timeframe in which the asset network must deliver services. These financial forecasts are:

In detail for the first three years of the programme

In outline for the next seven years of the programme

In less specific terms over the period for which the organisation has a strategic plan

The compilation of financial forecasts in the AMP is consistent, reliable and provable and these forecasts are reflected in the organisation's financial plans and budgets

Forecasts' sensitivities to potential significant changes in assumptions are analysed and discussed in the AMP and spreads of forecast expenditures are included where and as appropriate.

17.a.viii. Planning assumptions and confidence levels

AMPs:

List all the assumptions and provisos under which the plan and financial forecasts are developed

Note key assumptions regarding am planning in the organisation's strategic plans

List all assumptions and provisos

State the degrees of confidence in and reliability of the data underpinning the AMP, differentiating between critical and non-critical assets. In particular this will cover:

The asset inventory

Data on asset condition

Data on asset performance

Demand/growth forecasts

On the basis of these indications, provide a level of precision for, or confidence in, the expenditure forecasts for the asset network.

17.a.ix. AM improvement programmes

AMPs, and overarching AM strategies are be formally revised at least every three years, and the timing of these revisions is linked to the organisation's strategic planning cycles.

AM planning is seen as a constantly evolving process, with underpinning AM systems constantly providing better information

The improvement plan comments generally on achievements against the previous plan, and formally reports against that plan's KPIs

AM planning states what needs to be done to improve AM processes and techniques:

The Improvement Programme outlines

The weak areas

How weak areas will be addressed

The timeframe over which the improvements will occur

The resources (people and financial) needed

KPIs for monitoring AM improvement

AM planning is undertaken by suitably qualified and experienced people

The AMP and the planning processes are independently peer reviewed.

17.b. Steps in Preparing An AMP

Of all the steps, the most important is Step 6, Use the AMP, followed by Step 7, Update the AMP.

17.c. Suggested AMP Structure

There is no single correct way to structure AMPs and many organisations have adopted formats that suit their individual needs or preferences. Whatever structure is followed, the AMP should be fully integrated into the corporate business planning framework and contain sufficient information to support and justify the long term works programmes and financial forecasts that are a key output of AM planning.

A suitable structure should provide a logical flow through the AM process from defining what is required (in terms of meeting levels of service and changing demands) through the AM strategies and decision-making processes to the financial implications and business AM strengthening initiatives.

If the AMP has many different audiences, a tiered Plan may be appropriate. For example, the Executive Summary targeted at Board/Elected Members/Public, the main body of Plan for Management and appendices available for technical staff and contractors. The following content is principally sourced from section 4.2.6 of the IIMM 2011 edition, but it does contain additional detail from previous editions of the IIMM and from experience in writing AMPs.

It is a good idea to liaise with finance and other engineering and non-engineering staff to ensure that the key AMP outputs (levels of service, expenditure forecasts, etc.) are in a consistent format and can be easily incorporated into financial budgeting and strategic planning processes.

17.c.i. Executive summary

It is useful if the executive summary is a brief stand-alone document, aimed at a non-technical reader, which provides an overview of the levels of service, growth forecasts, key AM issues, significant works programmes and financial forecasts.

Some authorities describe the Executive Summary as the AMP and adopt it as such, with the sections described below becoming supporting appendices to the Plan, This has the advantage of reducing the overall size of the AMP itself, with consequent advantages to many readers It is a valid methodology but care needs to be taken that the AMP is not too summarised. The Executive Summary should include:

The AMPs purpose

The intended audience and target level of AM maturity

Corporate objectives

Corporate assumptions
Asset description
LoS
Future demand
Lifecycle management plan
Financial summary
AM practices
Monitoring and improvement programme.

17.c.ii. Section 1: Introduction

The Introduction provides an overview of all the elements of the network assets within the plan. It should also provide readers with a sound justification for the organisation owning and operating the assets covered, and the reasons for preparing the AMP.

Background:
Purpose of the Plan
The intended audience and target level of AM maturity
Relationship with other planning documents
Infrastructure assets included in the Plan
Key stakeholders in the Plan
Organisation structure
Corporate assumptions.
Goals and objectives of asset ownership, including reasons and justification for asset ownership and links to organisation vision, mission, goals and objectives
Plan framework
Core and advanced AM maturity and limitations of this plan.

17.c.iii. Section 2: Levels of service and delivery standards

LoS are essentially the standards for delivery – customer and technical service LoS and performance measures. This section of the plan identifies the current LoS being provided, confirms the basis for their adoption and describes how the LoS expectations of customers will be met.

Asset managers are not completely free to decide what to include, as the Local Government Act 2002 has some requirements that affect what is included in an AMP:

Section 2 of Schedule 10 states:

A long-term plan must, in relation to each group of activities of the local authority,—...

(d) include ...—

in detail in relation to each of the first 3 financial years covered by the plan; and

in outline in relation to each of the subsequent financial years covered by the plan.

Section 4 of the schedule states:

4 A long-term plan must, in relation to each group of activities of the local authority, include a statement of the intended levels of service provision that specifies—

any performance measures specified in a rule ...

the performance measures that the local authority considers will enable the public to assess the level of service ...; and

the performance target or targets set by the local authority for each performance measure; and

any intended changes to the level of service ...; and

the reason for any material change to the cost of a service.

The LoS section should include:

The services provided

Who uses or has interests in these services customers (including customer segmentation) and stakeholder's strategic and corporate goals

Customer research and expectations – how the LoS were

developed
Legislative requirements

Current LoS
Desired/proposed LoS and associated performance measures. It can be useful to include charts or tables showing the performance history
If not included elsewhere in the AMP, performance against agreed LoS.
Local authority AMPs should include this information in sufficient detail to meet the requirements of the LGA 2002 detailed above.
17.c.iv. Section 3: Future demand
This section should provide details of growth forecasts that affect the management and utilization of assets. Its objective is to identify factors and trends influencing demand for an asset and the effects of these on the asset management and utilization. Examples of factors and trends that may affect the future demand for an asset include:
Basic increases in demand – population growth, traffic growth, traffic type
Changes in unit demand – higher propensity to travel
Changes in customer expectations – faster vehicles, more safety, less delay, smoother travel, better signs.
The effect of the trends is quantified in terms of the effect on the growth of the network and the need to either increase or decrease infrastructure, or implement non-asset solutions through demand management.
The future demand section should include:
Demand drivers – factors influencing demand - anticipated changes in customer expectations, changes in technology,

population changes, economic changes, etc.

Demand forecasts – details of projected growth or decline of demands on services

Demand impacts on assets – ability of system to cope and changes in demand for the existing facilities

Demand management plan – how the changed demand will be met including through new facilities and demand management

Asset programmes to meet demand – major programmes or investigations and costs.

17.c.v. Section 4: Risk management

Although the IIMM suggests risk management be included in the Lifecycle Management section of the AMP many practitioners include it as a separate section because of its significance and the influences risk management has on the decisions made in the Lifecycle section.

Infrastructure risk management is the process of identifying risks than may affect the on-going delivery of services by that infrastructure. The Risk Management Plan should include:

Broad risk management strategies

Risk context (probability, consequence, risk-rating tables)

Summary of significant risks (the actual rating will depend on your corporate classification system) and management strategies

Either a reference to details in Risk Register/Risk Management Plan etc, or a risk analysis should be included. It should cover asset failure risks, operational risks, natural hazards, environmental risks and organisational risks. The template identified in NZS 4360 (Risk Management Standard) should be followed.

The discussion on Risk in Section 2.7 above and the

RIMS," Best-practice Guidelines for risk management on road networks", linked from that section provide good background for preparing a Risk Management Plan.

17.c.vi. Section 5: Lifecycle management

Lifecycle Management Plans are the "heart" of the AMP and cover the management strategies used to provide the desired LoS, taking into account the future changes in demand. The Lifecycle

Management section should outline how the assets are managed and operated to deliver the agreed LoS at the lowest lifecycle costs. It may be necessary to divide the network into separate geographic service areas (e.g. urban and rural roads) and/or to focus on each significant group (e.g. pavements, bridges, culverts, drainage, lighting etc.).

organisation of the lifecycle management

The two usual ways to present this information are by:

Arranging it by asset element

Arranging it by asset activity.

The approach adopted will be determined by the organization.

Asset element

This is the more traditional approach. Each sub-asset of element of the asset is discussed in a logical order and everything that is done in managing that element is detailed. For example:

Pavements

Carriageway surface

Maintenance and operations

Renewal

New surfaces

Disposal
Base course
Sub-base
Formation
Drainage.
Asset activity
This approach, which has largely been developed since the introduction of the Local Government Act 2002, is to consider all the activities that take place on the network and then describe those aspects of the management of the sub-asset management. For example:
Maintenance and operations
Formation
Pavement
Carriageway surface
Sealed surfaces
Metal surfaces.
Renewals
Formation
Pavement
Carriageway surface
Sealed surfaces
Metal surfaces
New works
Sub-categories as above
Disposals
Sub-categories as above.
content of the lifecycle management Section background data
There are two common approaches to including asset data. One is to describe the network and its high-level overview data in a separate section, usually immediately before or

after the LoS section. This approach "paints a picture" of either the assets available to provide the LoS, or the assets used to provide the LoS, and depends on whether the data comes before or after the LoS section. If this approach is used, the Lifecycle Management section can then supplement it with greater levels of detail and analysis of the asset data. The second approach is to provide the summary-level data in the early part of lifecycle section with greater levels of detail and analysis provided as the section progresses. This includes:

Physical parameters (including asset numbers)

General comments on the assets used, including a description of asset system, what it comprises, the land it is on, critical assets

How the system works

The asset mix, ages, sizes, materials, locations, and current issues

Summary of total asset parameters in table or graph formats, i.e. age distribution, size, what the assets are worth (asset valuations) etc.

An overall plan of asset system or network.

Asset capacity and performance

Design capacity, actual measured capacity and current utilisation of assets. Summary of details and statistics (e.g. percentage and distribution of assets under-capacity if known) related to the target LoS.

Refer to location of detailed information (e.g. traffic data, inventory information, calculations and analyses).

Asset condition

Summary of current asset condition, based on the best information currently available

Brief details on how condition is monitored

Age and condition information and/or profile graphs.

Asset valuations

If they are not included in the AMPs Financial Summary section, the following asset valuation information should be included:

Valuation summary by key component – replacement cost, depreciated replacement cost DRC, and annual depreciation

Description of valuation method

Basis for determining effective lives used for valuation

Key assumptions made in preparing valuation

Explanation for major changes from previous valuations.

historical data

Summary of historical data available, its type and location

Relevant historical financial information (historical trends etc.).

Infrastructure risk management plan

If there is not a separate Risk Management Section in the AMP then risk management should be covered here.

AM lifecycle strategies and plans

Each of the sub-sections should have clear and obvious links to the analyses described above, to asset condition and performance and with the plans and other interventions developed.

Routine operations and maintenance

Routine operations and maintenance are the normal day-to-day works that are necessary to keep assets operating, including instances where portions of the asset fail and need immediate repair to make the asset operational again. This sub-section should include discussion of:

Operations and Maintenance Strategies

Describing the maintenance and operations strategies and methods used to deliver the required LoS. This should include how the divisions between planned and reactive maintenance tasks are optimised

Describing how maintenance tasks are prioritised

Discussing the risks, including LoS risks, associated with alternative maintenance standards

Operations and Maintenance Plan

Outlining the decision-making process for planned and reactive maintenance

Discussing trends (e.g. issues, past spend, complaints)

Listing assumptions and uncertainties underlying and in the programme

Summarising future costs

Local authorities in New Zealand are required to forecast their financial needs in detail for the first three years of each long-term plan and in outline for the balance9. Forecasts should provide the information in sufficient detail to meet this need.

A forecast operations and maintenance costs for planned and reactive work should be included

Any deferred maintenance should be identified and included and the associated risk identified.

Asset renewal and replacement

Asset renewal and replacement is major work which restores, rehabilitates, replaces or renews an existing asset to its original capacity or to a state in which it can deliver its original LoS, but is not designed to increase its capacity or the LoS it delivers. This sub-section should include discussion of:

Renewal strategies

Describing the decision-making process for asset renewals including how they are identified and prioritised and to what standards assets are replaced (e.g. types of failure, options for treatment, risk, etc.)

Describing the renewal strategies, methods to meet required LoS

Discussing the risks, including LoS risks, associated with alternative renewal standards

The Renewal Plan, detailing:

The forecast renewal/replacement programme based on projected ends of life. Costs and projects should be in detail for the first three years of each long-term plan and in outline for the balance10;

Identifying and including any deferred renewals

The assumptions and uncertainties in the programme.

Creation, acquisition and augmentation

Creation or acquisition of new assets and improvements in LoS are described in numerous ways. In this section all are covered by the term "new works". New works are those that create a new asset that did not previously exist, to upgrade or improve an existing asset beyond its existing capacity to provide a new or improved LoS. New works may result from growth, social or environmental needs or decisions to improve the LoS to existing customers. This sub-section should include discussion about:

Asset creation/capital investment strategies, including:

The asset creation decision-making processes

Descriptions of any specific strategies or methods to meet anticipated improvements in LoS, including how the needs for new or augmented assets are identified and prioritised, and to what standards they are built

Descriptions of any Demand Management Strategies or practices and the place of demand management in reducing, deferring or removing the need to create new assets

Details of the risks, including LoS risks, associated with alternative asset creation strategies and standards, including demand management

Descriptions of the formal procedures used to rank asset creation/acquisition projects

Outlines of the methods and practices used to ensure that new assets created by, or for (e.g. by land developers) the organisation best meet its needs and are completed on time to the required standard and cost. These should cover:

Value management during design phase; procedures and criteria for assessment of design options (including consideration of lifecycle costs, optimised renewal decision making and risk assessment)

Project management procedures project review

Quality assurance and audit trails for design and project management

Risks associated with alternatives and how these will be managed

The Asset Creation/Augmentation Plan, detailing:

Assumptions and uncertainties in the programme

The forecast Asset Improvement Programme including:

The forecast Asset Improvement Programme. Costs and projects should be in detail for the first three years of each long-term plan and in outline for the balance11

Future needs for acquisition and/or purchase of assets based on demand forecasts

Identifying how the costs of new assets will be funded.

Disposal plan

Disposal is any of the activities associated with removal of an asset from service or removal of the LoS provided by an asset, including decommissioning, sale, demolition, relocation or permanent reduction in LoS. This sub-section should include discussion of:

Asset disposal strategies, including:

Details of any legislative constraints on asset disposal (e.g. Road Stopping legislation)

Descriptions of any asset disposal strategies or methods to meet anticipated improvements in LoS

Descriptions of how disposals are identified, prioritised and approved

Details of any disposals driven by demand management strategies, including summaries of each justification

Descriptions of the risks, including LoS risks, associated with each disposal and the alternatives to it

A discussion of the methods used to ensure that disposal of an asset does not create problems or additional unanticipated costs for the organisation or its customers. These should cover:

Procedures and criteria for assessment of options (including consideration of direct and indirect costs, maintenance of public health and public safety, optimised decision making and assessment of the risks associated with the proposed disposal, its alternatives and how these risks will be managed;

Project management procedures, project review, quality assurance and audit trails as applicable;

Asset Disposal Plan including:

Discussion of the disposals planned, covering the factors

resulting from consideration of the strategy's factors
Demonstration of the needs to dispose of assets and description of the standards to against which each disposal is assessed
Identification of how disposal of assets will be funded and how any net income will be treated
The forecast Asset Disposal Programme including:
Forecast disposals of assets including timing, costs and income. Costs and projects should be in detail for the first three years of each long-term plan and in outline for the balance12
Identification of how the costs of asset disposals will be funded.
17.c.vii. Section 6: Financial summary
Local authorities' financial forecasts are governed by the LGA 2002. The NZTA's Highway and Network division has similar requirements under the Government Roading Powers Act 198913 and all RCA's have to comply with The NZTA's procedures and requirements established under the Land Transport Management Act 2003.
This section should contain the financial requirements resulting from information presented in previous sections. As AMPs become more advanced, various LoS and cost scenarios may be included. As detailed above, local authorities are required to prepare and publish their programmes in detail for three years and in outline for the balance of the Long Term Plan period (at least a further seven years). These published programmes should be linked to the lifecycle management plans and cover operational, maintenance, renewal, creation and disposal costs. Detail should include the following. The asset valuation may be included here rather than in the Lifecycle

Management section.

Summary of relevant Financial Policies

This should inform the reader of the relevant financial policies that influence the management of and accounting for the assets covered by the Plan. It should include:

Financial management policies (depreciation, disposals, etc.)

Funding policies:

Debt/revenue funding

User charges

Development contributions.

Funding Strategy

This should include:

Provide details of how expenditure will be treated financially (e.g. capitalisation policies) and funded.

Describe how and by whom any needs to smooth out variations in cash flow are determined and implemented.

Financial Statements And Projections

These should be prepared for in detail for the first three years and in outline for at least a further seven years and include:

Cash flow forecasts by year, in formats (e.g. maintenance, renewal and new works) that meet the requirements and needs of the organisation's finance managers

Revenue/income forecast. If revenue is not included in the financial forecasts in the Lifecycle Management Plans, a revenue forecast should be included

Breakdown of expenditure by service groups

Trends from the previous two to three years

Although the LGA does not require the effects of inflation to be included in financial forecasts, the Auditor General does. Section 2.8.2 above discusses a practical way of meeting this need while retaining the advantages of a constant-dollar budget.

valuation Forecasts

These should include:

Forecasts of the future value of asset and a description of the valuation methodology used to develop these

Forecasts of depreciation.

key Assumptions made in Financial Forecasts

These should include:

The key assumptions made in preparing the forecasts, the confidence levels associated with those assumptions and the risks if these assumptions change

Readers should understand the accuracy of the information presented as well as receiving an insight as to how the organisation intends to improve the accuracy of future financial forecasts

Advanced AMPs may also include a sensitivity analysis quantifying variations in the forecasts resulting from possible scenarios relating to key assumptions.

17.c.viii. Section 7: AM practices, plan monitoring and the AM improvement plan

The AM Practices, Plan Improvement and Monitoring section describes, identifies and prioritises the tasks that will contribute to the improvement of the organisation's AM practices. It must not be confused with the Asset Improvement Plan which describes new works/development/asset improvements. It should give the reader an understanding of:

How AM decisions are made

Current asset management performance

Proposed improvements to AM systems and practices that

will address deficiencies or improve the level of confidence in the AMP

The programme for implementing the improvements – i.e., the AM Improvement Plan.

The AM Improvement Plan itself should give the reader an understanding of how and when AM practices will be improved, and the resources required to do so. It should also:

Provide details on planning for monitoring the performance of the AMP and of any improvements to AM systems that will improve the level of confidence in the AMP

Detail the Improvement Programme listing:

The actions proposed

Resources required

Priorities and timings

Responsibilities for each improvement.

This section should, like all the other programmes in the AMP, be in detail for the first three years and in outline for the balance of the programme.

Suggested contents include:

Current and desired states of AM processes, data, systems and performance

Management practices

The customer interface

Contract management

Support processes needed to support effective lifecycle AM

Data collection and analysis

System monitoring and reporting

Key systems (AMIS, GIS, SCADA, etc.)

Quality assurance, including works, contract management,

data collection and all other aspects of asset management
AM Performance (as distinct from the performance of the assets themselves):
Describing how the effectiveness of the AMP will be measured (AM Performance Measures)
Showing achieved AM performance against the measures detailed. It can be useful to include charts or tables showing the performance history
Monitoring and Review Procedures
Procedures and timetable for performance reporting
AMP review cycle (three-yearly review of AMP)
Timetable for external audit and review (of process, data integrity, LoS)
Improvement Plan
Prioritised summary of all the improvements identified for the Plan, including improvements to content, and data availability, accuracy and confidence
Improvement Programme including details of actions proposed, resources required, timings and responsibility for each improvement outlined in the summary. This programme should, like all the other programmes in the AMP, be in detail for the first three years and outline for the balance of the programme.
Implementing Asset management Plans And managing changes to Asset
18.a. implementation
There are two extremely important steps required to implement any infrastructural AMP. They are to:
Adopt the Plan
Use it.
18.b. Adoption
While an AMP can be useful to the writer as soon as it is

written, its usefulness and influence are severely limited if does not have any status as a corporate document. As soon as it is adopted the AMP it has the status of "Corporate Policy" and its ability to influence what and why decisions are made and how they affect the assets is significantly increased. Its procedures and forecasts gain similar status and the AMP itself becomes an authoritative reference.

Most experienced asset managers therefore consider it essential for AMPs to be put before the board of directors or full council for debate and adoption.

18..c. Use

All the work and effort put into preparing and adopting an AMP is wasted unless it is used. "Use it" is therefore the most important step in the whole process:

Refer to it regularly

Make it the prime source of information on the management of the asset, including the place where approved budgets and programmes are to be found and copies of strategies influencing the asset are stored

Ensure that LoS are incorporated into maintenance contracts, renewal contracts and contracts for new and improvement works at the earliest possible opportunities. If it is practical and possible

to do so, introduce any necessary contractual changes by way of variations rather than waiting for the next contract to start

Implement the AM Improvement Plan.

18.d. Changes to assets

Individual assets and the data describing them are subject to continuous change, through wear and tear, maintenance activities, renewal, the creation of new works and

improvements by the asset owner or by others.
As good accurate asset information is necessary for AM it is essential that the RCA puts in place sound, practical procedures for the timely, accurate and efficient collection of all the data that has changed and all the new data it needs as a result of these changes. It is useful to prepare a standard document detailing data requirements.

It is also important to determine when updated data will be collected. The most common options are:
On occurrence
At fixed intervals, often annually, in batches.
Batch-collection is often promoted as being more efficient, and this can be the case if non-local contracted staff are used, but the apparent efficiencies of this approach tend to be offset by:
The issues caused by having incorrect data while waiting for the updates to occur. These include:
Imprecise and non-documented details of new assets that must nevertheless be maintained and managed
Incorrect condition details and other attributes for existing assets. These may result in unnecessary despatches to fix issues that have been resolved
The efficiencies possible by using modern technologies such as 'Pocket RAMM' to simplify and expedite the data collection processes, allowing local staff to collect data and to do so quickly and without the necessity for extensive planning and preparation.
In addition to recording visible data, it is essential the necessary information is collected on hidden assets and invisible asset data. This should include items such as layer

or material thickness, retaining walls supporting the road but not readily apparent from it, creation dates, material source or type, manufacturer and model numbers (especially for assets such as lighting and traffic signals, ornamental bollards, guard-rail terminals etc.).

18.e. Vested assets

These are the assets that are created by others and become the RCA's property when the development is handed over. It is too late to object to the design or other non-conforming aspects of a vested work when it is complete and being handed over. To avoid problems caused by the creation of sub-standard or "gold-plated"14 assets, it is essential that the asset manager or a trusted delegate be included in the subdivision/vested asset approval process at all stages, including:

Concept discussions

Examination of proposals

Vetting of resource and planning consent applications before submission

Statutory and other approvals

Checking and approval of detailed construction drawings and all specifications

All construction supervision

Inspections at practical completion

Final inspections at the end of the maintenance periods.

Achieving this level of involvement, and the goals it seeks, can be significantly assisted by adopting the AMP at the highest possible level in the organisation.

continuous improvement

Most RCAs have moved, or are moving, towards advanced AM. Basic AM, based on current LoS, no longer meets legislative requirements or Audit NZ guidelines for many activities, especially roading. Advanced AM moves to incorporate service level reviews and optimising strategies, including predictive modelling, risk management, and optimised decision making.

This said, it may not be appropriate or cost-effective for an authority to attain and maintain full Advanced AM capabilities. The level of AM maturity adopted by an organisation and reflected in its AMPs and practices should be appropriate, practical and affordable. In the United States the Association of American State Highway Officials (AASHTO) has adopted a more finely graduated scale of AM maturity than the "Basic and Advanced" one that has developed in New Zealand. It may be helpful to consider the AASHTO scale when looking at the appropriate level of AM maturity an organisation aspires to. Its AM maturity levels are:

Table 19 1: AASHTO AM maturity scale.

To achieve proficient or advanced AM organisations need to be able to demonstrate the following:

Knowledge of asset ownership;

Knowledge of LoS

Ability to predict future demand from customers

Knowledge of physical condition of assets

Knowledge of performance of assets

Knowledge of current utilisation and ultimate capacity

Ability to predict failure modes of assets

Ability to analyse alternative treatment options

Ability to rank works based on economic analysis

Ability to rationalise works based on available budget

Ability to develop and revise strategic objectives for each

asset
Ability to optimise operations and maintenance activities.
To achieve best practice status an organization must be among the leaders in these areas.
AM maturity does not suddenly change in significant steps, as might be suggested by Table 6 1. Rather, it happens continually and often un-noticed. It is therefore necessary to plan the
management of changes to management practices, just as we plan for the management of the changes that occur to the assets themselves.
19.a. Formal AMP review
A powerful method for driving and influencing changes in an AMP to bring it up to date with an organisation's current practices and align it more closely with its goals is to carry out a formal structured review of the AMP and AM Practices.
There are a number of proprietary systems that form the bases for these evaluations. The following table is indicative of the AM elements assessed. In the example illustrated there are five or more criteria examined for each asset element, in each of which current practice and the organisation's desired practice are scored and can be assessed against a benchmark.
Table 19.1 1: Typical AMP review elements.

Asset category

Asset element

Asset Knowledge
Asset Categorization

Asset Life Data

Capacity Data

Condition Data

Financial Data

Location Data

Operations and Maintenance (O&M)Data

Performance Data

Physical Attributes Data

Risk Management Data

Asset Management Plan
AMP AM Practices and Improvement to them

AMP Asset Data and Descriptions

AMP Demand Forecasting and Management

AMP General

AMP LoS

AMP Lifecycle Strategies

AMP Long Term Financial Plans

Asset category

Asset element

Asset Management Practices
CAPEX Contract Management

CAPEX Evaluation

Design Processes

O & M Contract Management

O & M Monitoring

O & M Plans

O & M Strategy and Analysis

Project Identification and Prioritisation

Business Culture
Innovation

LoS Management

Managing for Quality

Risk Management

Senior Leadership

Social Responsibility

Human Resources
Employee Education and Training

Employee Involvement

Employee Performance and Recognition

Employee Satisfaction

HR Planning and Management

Information Systems
Advanced AM Systems

Asset Register System

Capacity or Utilisation Models

Maintenance Management System

Spatial Information System

Legislative Compliance
AM Practices

Community Outcomes

Financial

Growth and Demand

Improvement Plan

Levels of Service

Life Cycle Management

Risk

Asset category

Asset element

Organizational Tactics
AM Improvement

AM Responsibilities

AM Training and Skills

Commercial Tactics

Corporate Objectives

Corporate Sponsorship and Commitment

Funding Strategy

Legislative Compliance

Strategic Planning Processes
Community Outcomes

Demand Forecasting Processes

Failure Prediction

Optimised Decision Making

Risk Management Strategy

Service Level Reviews

Sustainability

Even if this level of external review is not undertaken it can be useful for another asset manager in the organisation or one in a friendly outside organisation to review the AMP before a rewrite is undertaken.
The output of any plan review should be either an agreed, or at least a suggested, list of improvements or changes to the reviewed plan, with immediate and longer term changes identified and the latter prioritised for inclusion in the revised AM Improvement Plan.

19.b. improvement of AM Plans And Practices
AMPs are dynamic documents and must be updated periodically to maintain relevance. Each AMP should be updated:
As your objectives or customer expectations change
As your AM systems improve
When key assumptions or strategies change

Whenever there is any other appreciable change that affects the asset, such as changes in legislation or adoption of a new policy

To prepare the financial plans for inclusion in each Long Term Plan and budget

To match adopted financial programmes when these are different to those in the AMP

When there are other significant changes to the organisation's goal, objectives, operating environment – including the legal environment in which it works, or financial situation

Ideally, in advance of major long-term maintenance contracts, so that the most appropriate LoS can be included in the contract documents without variation.

AM improvement activities that will be incorporated into future plans should be continual between plan updates.

19.c. Asset maintenance, renewal and construction practice changes

Changes to why work is carried out, what is done and when, are themselves areas of continuous change. Many potential changes are claimed to reduce lifecycle costs but these claims need to be subject to rigorous scrutiny before adoption. Often, if achievement of lower lifecycle costs is not possible when the technology or practice is introduced, it can be achieved as it matures and initial costs decline. It is therefore essential for both contractors and asset managers to keep abreast of changes to practices, materials and equipment to allow the appropriate reaction at the most suitable time.

19.d. AM Improvement considerations

A typical improvement plan is developed through consideration of the following steps or processes:

Current and desired states of AM processes, data and systems

Management practices

Customer interfaces

Contracts management

Quality assurance

Support processes:

Key systems (AMIS, GIS, SCADA, etc.)

Data collection

System monitoring

AMP

Content

Layout

Data availability, accuracy and confidence

AM Performance

AM Performance Measures outlining how the effectiveness and performance of the AM system will be measured

Achieved AM performance against the measures detailed. It can be useful to include charts or tables showing the performance history

Monitoring and Review Procedures

Procedures and timetable for performance reporting

AMP review cycle

Timetable for external audit and review (of process, data integrity, LoS).

The Importance of Asset Management in the Transportation Business

An asset is the wealth owned by a company. Good form in the form of land, machinery, bonds, stocks, vehicles, and all objects that have value and can be guaranteed if at any time needed. Good asset management keeps the company's revenue growth at maximum performance. A well-functioning company asset will deliver the company to targets that will be achieved in the future.

Maintaining the Quality of Assets to Stay Good

In the transportation business such as taxis, motorbikes, shuttle bus, logistics, aircraft, and ship, transportation equipment owned by the company is a valuable asset.

Implementing asset management with periodically controlled vehicle service will keep the performance of the vehicle capable, avoiding vehicles from damage that causes asset value to decrease, decreasing the performance of vehicles that have an impact on service decline, and also causes a decrease in income.

Optimizing Company Finance

Asset management is needed for companies to see the performance of their vehicles. The use of software in asset management that is able to measure fuel use in one vehicle while also measuring the odometer of a vehicle, will greatly help companies to take care of the vehicles they have.

Having complete data on how much fuel is needed by a vehicle for certain distance units makes it easy for companies to estimate daily or monthly costs.

In addition, data on vehicle mileage through tracking vehicle odometers can also help companies carry out better asset management, for example, to find out when engine oil must be replaced, for every thousand kilometers the tire must be replaced with a new one when the brake lining must be replaced.

For each how much distance the electricity in the vehicle

must be checked, and for the journey to what extent the radiator water must be replenished, etc.. All of this data will then lead to budget estimates that must be prepared by the company each month.

Control of Decreasing Asset Value

A decline in asset value is very common for fixed assets such as vehicles. The year of production, usage period, and technological development are the supporting factors for the decline in vehicle asset value.

For this reason, the implementation of asset management in the company will make it easier for companies to monitor the decline in the value of their assets. Thus, it will help companies in budgeting for asset purchases in the future.

Debriefing on Vehicle Drivers

Maintaining vehicle asset management does not only apply to all parts attached to the vehicle, but also to the driver. Understanding the driver is a matter of how the working system of a vehicle engine, what distance must be taken by the vehicle before finally the oil must be replaced, and how much fuel is used for one trip.

How many thousand kilometers must be taken by the vehicle until the tire has to replace. The general knowledge that must be owned by the driver.

The knowledge possessed by drivers will be very much needed if sudden damage occurs so that the driver can take the necessary action quickly. By providing knowledge about the vehicle that he uses, it will create a sense of security for customers and can realize maximum service.

Helping Company Management in Making Decisions

Asset management enables dialogue between company directors, asset management managers, and daily operational workers.

This dialog will be created when all parties gain access to view all data from the asset management report. This data will be very useful for company management in making decisions in terms of managing assets that they have.

Good Risk Management

Asset management transportation helps companies keep their vehicles operating optimally. Vehicles that operate optimally will guarantee that drivers and their passengers are safe whiles on the road.

This will prevent the company from the risk of accidents that have a negative impact on customer trust in the company on the one hand and on the other hand, have an impact on decreasing income.

More Guarded Company Assets

Utilization of asset management software from HashMicro in a transportation company, helps you track where your vehicle is, what route it travels, and how far the distance and time it takes. That way you can supervise your assets and make your assets safer.

Table of Contents

A Comprehensive Guide to Strategies, Practices and Benchmarking. 1

6.1. Elements of asset integrity management. 4

6.2. The human element. 5

6.3. Plugging the gaps in asset integrity management systems. 6

6.4. Why asset integrity management is important. 6

6.5. Constructing an AIM strategy. 6

6.7. RBI: risk-based inspection. 7

6.8. dentifying damage conditions - and the factors that alter them.. 7
9.1. Fixed Equipment Inspection and Certification. 10
9.2. Corrosion Under Insulation. 10
12.1 Demand management. 13
12.2 Maintenance management. 14
12.3. Renewal management. 16
12.4. Management of improvements and new work needs. 16
13.1 Identification of critical assets. 17
13.2 Risk treatment. 17
13.3 Risk prioritisation. 18
13.4 Outputs from risk analysis process. 19
14.1 Financial linkages. 19
14.2 Inflation. 21
14.3 Forecasting approach. 22
16.b.i. New works and improvements links. 26
16.b.ii. Maintenance and operations links. 28
Renewals and rehabilitation links. 29
Disposals links. 29
16.c.i. Forecasting NZTA Financial Assistance. 31
16.c.ii. Forecasting financial and development-contribution incomes. 32
16.c.iii. Forecasting income from fees and charges. 32
16.c.iv. Forecasting loans. 32
16.c.v. Other aspects of planning funding of roading activities. 32
17.a.i. Organisational recognition. 33
17.a.ii. Levels of service. 34
17.a.iii. Asset knowledge. 34
17.a.iv. Growth management (positive or negative). 34
17.a.v. Risk management. 35

17.a.vi. Optimised decision-making. 35
17.a.vii. Financial forecasts. 35
17.a.viii. Planning assumptions and confidence levels. 35
17.a.ix. AM improvement programmes. 36
17.c.i. Executive summary. 39
17.c.ii. Section 1: Introduction. 39
17.c.iii. Section 2: Levels of service and delivery standards. 40
17.c.iv. Section 3: Future demand. 41
17.c.v. Section 4: Risk management. 41
17.c.vi. Section 5: Lifecycle management. 42
17.c.vii. Section 6: Financial summary. 47
17.c.viii. Section 7: AM practices, plan monitoring and the AM improvement plan. 48
18.b. Adoption. 50
18..c. Use. 50
18.d. Changes to assets. 50
18.e. Vested assets. 51
19.c. Asset maintenance, renewal and construction practice changes. 56
19.d. AM Improvement considerations. 56
Optimizing Company Finance. 58
Control of Decreasing Asset Value. 59
Debriefing on Vehicle Drivers. 59
Helping Company Management in Making Decisions. 60
Good Risk Management. 60

Start writing...

www.ingramcontent.com/pod-product-compliance
Lightning Source LLC
La Vergne TN
LVHW100335181026
850499LV00039B/1088
* 9 7 8 9 3 5 4 5 8 3 3 1 5 *